Crouch

AMERICAN
CUT GLASS

By

EDWIN G. WARMAN

A Pattern Book of the Brilliant Period
1895-1915

NINTH PRINTING AUGUST, 1968

E. G. WARMAN PUBLISHING INC.
UNIONTOWN PENNSYLVANIA

*Additional copies of his book may be purchased
from your book dealer; or, orders may be
sent directly to the publisher.*

Price $4.75 Per Copy

E. G. WARMAN PUBLISHING INC.
8 FRANKHOOVER STREET
UNIONTOWN. PENNA.

Printed in the United States of America

24349

- INTRODUCTION -

A revival of interest in Cut Glass has become apparent within the last few years. Antique
dealers report that sales, as well as the number
of collectors, have increased.

The majority of Cut Glass offered for sale
in Antique Shops today is of the "Brilliant Period"
(1895-1915). As the supply of prime antiques dimin-
ishes, collectors turn to new fields, which are in
the "collector category"--as is Cut Glass.

Collectors and dealers have been handicapped
in the Cut Glass field because of the lack of
classifications of patterns in the late period.
The purpose of this pattern book is to fill that
need.

With the passing of time, Cut Glass is now
considered a "collectible" just as pattern glass
is at the moment. The greater part of the design
was cut by hand and each piece showed individual-
ity rather than the "mass production" appearance
of pattern glass.

Cut Glass was expensive when new. It was not
a poor man's commodity. The design entered into
the selling price for the finer and more intricate
the design, the higher the value.

It is unlikely that Cut Glass will ever again
be made in quantity, for the present day cost would
be at least three times that of the original. Then,
too, the period has passed and the general public
is no longer interested, which leaves the field to
the collectors.   Edwin G. Warman,
                                      Uniontown, Penna.

HISTORY OF CUT GLASS

The origin of glassmaking is obscure and lost among ancient historical records. Pliny and Strabo A.D. 23, give accurate accounts of the glasshouses in Sidon and Alexandria. This proves that not only was the manufacture of glass known at that early period, but also that methods of cutting, engraving and coloring were practiced. Mummies in Egypt, more than 3000 years old, have been found with glass beads, which carries the manufacture of glass to remote times.

In Rome, the manufacture of glass was introduced when Cicero lived. Excavations have revealed that many types of vessels, vases and other household articles were in common use.

One of the most celebrated ancient works in glass is the Barberini or Portland vase, found in the tomb of Alexander Severus, who died A.D. 235. The vase was bought in 1786, by the Duke of Portland and loaned to the British Museum.

Any incisory form of ornamenting glass with diamond or hard metal point by a lapidary's wheel was usually described by early historians as being "cut." The first Cut Glass of which we have knowledge was made in Rome. Examples of the work are well represented in the British Museum.

Roman cutters appear to have been succeeded by craftsmen in Constantinople. After the fall of Constantinople to the Turks in 1453, there was a renaissance of glass cutting in Italy. At the end of the 16th. Century, Rudolph II, induced Italian cutters from Milan to work in the Crystal and glass cutting factory which he established at Prague. Specimens of this Bohemian glass found their way to England. However, there is no record of English Cut Glass before the beginning of the 18th. Century.

By 1713, English Cut Glass began appearing on the Continent of Europe. In 1760, England was supplying practically the whole of France and other parts of Europe with this type of glass. Thus a deadly blow was dealt to the colorless Bohemian type. The superiority of English lead glass to the Bohemian glass lay not only in the purity of the metal, but in its density and brilliance.

Ireland followed England in glass cutting. By 1750, a thriving industry was well established in Cork, Dublin and Waterford. The English factories were hurt by this competition, and in 1788 the English Parliament passed an Act prohibiting the export of glass from Ireland entirely. This measure crippled the thriving industry in Ireland.

The cutting of glass in America is first attributed to "Baron" Henry William Stiegel, of Manheim, Pennsylvania, about 1772. Next, cutting was practiced to some extent at the Amelung glass works, located near Frederick, Maryland. The workmen at these plants were German emigrants and closely followed the "Continental" types and methods of production. The later American factories followed the English and Irish standards of production in the early years following 1800.

An exerpt from a letter written Dec. 17, 1836 by an official of Bakewells & Co., Pittsburgh, Penna., to W. G. Lyford follows: "We have pursued the business in this city for nearly thirty years and have had the honor of making sets of glass for two Presidents of the United States; of making a set of splendid vases of Cut Glass to adorn the salon of General Lafayette at LaGrange; of having received the silver medal awarded by the Franklin institute for the best speciman of Cut Glass."

The Cut Glass which was made in America can be divided into three periods, namely: "Early," "Middle" and "Brilliant." The Glass of the first two periods is in the rare class and very few examples are available in Antique Shops today. "American Cut Glass" deals with the "Brilliant" period.

The "Brilliant Period" had its beginning in the late 1880's, when the pattern glass era was nearing its peak. The mass production of Pattern glass made it available to practically every home. The cultured and wealthy class turned away from it because it became cheap and common. Cut Glass became a mark of distinction when shown and used by the discriminating hostess. It was expensive and exclusive--well above the financial range of persons of ordinary means. During the period 1895-1915, the glass was considered a "must" for weddings, anniversaries and other important occasions of gift giving.

Shortly after 1900, new methods of cutting and polishing were discovered. The glass became less expensive to purchase but was never as cheap as pattern glass. Around 1910, the wealthy class lost interest and by the beginning of World War I, the public interest in Cut Glass was supplanted by the war effort. Glass cutters turned to lens and prism making. European imports were no longer received and the country in general was in a state of anxiety and tension. People moved to the cities as industry expanded.

In this chaotic period much of the glass was relegated to attics and barns, some was lost and destroyed. The conclusion of the war marked the end of "mass interest" in Cut Glass.

The glass lay dormant from 1920, except for an occasional showing, or use, until 1950, when collectors in their desire to discover something new, turned to these early holdings.

Collectors have discovered that the fine workmanship required to produce the glass cannot be duplicated today because of the lack of workmen and the cost involved. A bowl selling for $15.00 in an Antique Shop today could not be reproduced for $50.00.

With the coming of collectors into the field, the need for a handbook of patterns has developed. The publication of "American Cut Glass" is not an attempt to record the history of individual patterns, but is presented as a "working tool" for collectors and dealers. Cut Glass patterns can now be identified and sold by name just as pattern glass is today.

GLASS CUTTING

The introduction of glass cutting into the art of glass decoration opened a new and lucrative commercial venture for the glass business. From 1880 to 1915, this branch of glassware grew and flourished in America. It is this particular period of time in which we are interested. Especially in the methods by which such cut glass was produced. Very little background history is needed here for we are interested primarily in the tools and processes that were needed to make and produce the various cuts on pieces of glassware.

A cutter of iron and steel, Casper Lehmann, is recorded as having discovered the art of cutting glass. Actually, he only redeveloped it. However, due to the lack of evidence, he was granted a patent on his process in the year of 1609, by the Emperor Rudolphus II, of Germany. Lehmann became the court lapidary and glass cutter, practicing his trade in the city of Prague.

It was not, however, until the beginning of the 18th. Century, in the city of Nuremburg, that the art of glass cutting began to grow as a practical business and industry. Later in England and afterwards in France, new developments were taking place in the making of raw glass which produced a superior type of glass suitable for decoration.

For all of the confused and voluminous material on the background of glass, it is curious just how meager is the information on the cutting of glass, and also just what cut glass really is.

11

Few people know how to tell cut glass from engraved glass; and others, in some instances, mistake well moulded pressed glass for cut. These mistakes even go so far as to be found in articles on glass, until it is extremely difficult to find a clear understanding of the subject.

Many stories tell of how methods of cutting glass employed emery powders and sharp pointed instruments of hardened steel as well as with heated irons. Actually these misinformations belong to the allied arts of engraving on glass, and the parting, slitting and splitting of glass.

The words of cut, engrave, carve, do not signify one and the same thing, but different things. Perhaps the word "cut" as referred to the flint glass trade is the meaning that is the safest to pursue and will be the avenue that we shall explore.

Pressed and moulded glass are sometimes mistaken for, and are made in imitation of, cut and other ornamental glass where geometrical design is used. These imitations are less brilliant, duller-edged, more rounded in pattern and, of course, less sparkling. Pressed glass is made, as its name implies, in presses which turn out large quantities rapidly.

Cut Glass is mainly distinguished from engraved, carved, etched and other ornamental glass by the geometrical lines of its patterns which form prisms and facets of generally four, six, and eight sides; and, also by lines which do not form prisms and facets.

The cutting shop of a cut glass plant consists of long rows of equipment known as frames, each of which carries between its two main side supports the removable spindles which bear the wheels of iron, stone, wood, leather and felt. These cutting and working machines are run by

steam engines or electric motors which revolve
a long shaft over the whole row of benches.
Individual belts are linked by pulleys to each
cutting table so that any of the machines can be
run independently of all the others at any time.
Modernization has caused some very revolutionary
equipment to be used today, but we are interested
primarily in the cut glass methods of the early
1900's.

In order to understand how cut glass is made
or cut, we must look at the cutter's tools. In
this manner the work is more understandable. The
cutting wheels, which are the primary tools used,
are made of iron and stone. Their sizes vary from
a quarter of an inch in thickness and two inches
in diameter to about one inch and a quarter in
thickness and twenty-five inches in diameter.
The finishing wheels of cork, wood, felt and
leather are seldom so large. The iron wheels do
not, as a rule, bear edges as sharp as those of
the stone. The stone, whether mitred or flat-
faced, corresponds to the iron wheels in their
surface shape.

Certain types of stone are better than others
for glass cutting. They are rough hewn in the
round when the cutter orders them. He must turn
them round and true them for the glass cutting
work later. This he does by fastening the rough
wheel on a spindle with a screw and nut, and then
turning it true with the aid of an iron bar with
wet sand held against it.

The uneven edges, sides and face are reduced
by this means to a smooth-going circle, and are
then "fined" (finished) up with hard stone and
flint. The "mills", or iron wheels, are generally
of wrought iron, though sometimes are made of
cast iron. They are turned true on a metal working
lathe. The turning tools are well-tempered flat or
three-cornered steel. The wood and cork are easy
to turn true. Once the wheels are made true they
are ready for use.

If a narrower rounded wheel is used, and the glass is drawn up and down in a line with the wheel's revolution, a "split" cut is the result. It is a deeper cut than the ordinary "flute" cut, which is produced by drawing the glass across the wheel, in line with the spindle.

This split cut wheel, if flattened on the face, becomes a "panel" wheel. Its cut is sharp-edged, like itself. The incision made by the wheel on the glass that is not intentionally moved in some way while receiving the incision, must be deeper in the middle than at any other part of it. The reason is that the cutting power of a wheel in motion is greatest at its nearest point of contact with the glass which is being cut. An incision any length that the glass will allow may be made on it by moving the glass in any given direction.

In rough cutting, a small stream of sand and water falls onto the wheel while it is in motion. From a sloping trough, this wet mixture falls onto the face of the wheel. It is the sand between the wheel and the glass that cuts the groove and not the wheel itself.

When the heavy work is done, the cutter or another workman, called a "smoother," passes the stone wheel—which is shaped on the face like the iron one but supplied only with water—into the cuts to smooth them. This operation gives them a better shape before the polishing is begun on the wooden wheel. A brush wheel dressed with wet ground pumice mixed with powdered rotten stone, or with moistened putty powder, is used when extra lustre is required.

To flute the leg, or stem, of a goblet, the cutter continues until the leg has all its flutes. These flutes are afterwards smoothed and polished.

The "hexagon diamond" pattern of some goblet bowls is cut with the mitre wheel. The sides of the mitre give form to the prisms as they sink into the sides of the glass. The prisms become the shoulders of the facets in this and in similar patterns. The square-sided stars which are sometimes seen in the borders, tops and bottoms of bowls are often well contrived. They would have taken their ordinary and natural round forms but for the stout little mitre cuts, done between each with a very small wheel, as well as the horizontal lines of the border, which square them into their places. The foot of a goblet can show very effective glass cutting. Scallops, when they appear, must be cut just the same as any other part of the design.

Three-sided, four-sided, six-sided and eight-sided prismy "diamond" patterns are produced by the use of the mitre wheel. The true prism of optics is a triangular-shaped piece of glass, or other transparent medium, with polished surfaces.

Mitre cuts lose the curves on their sides and become angular when made up against the sides of other mitre cuts. Cutters strive for various arrangements of angle cuts. The points may be cut off of any of them with the mitre tool and their shapes varied accordingly. If the four points of such a diagram are cut away, an eight-sided design remains. This design has become known as the "octagon diamond" and is used extensively. When arranged at equal distances on the straight body of a decanter or a vase; or, when made to vary in size with the narrowing towards the neck or foot, they show between them the thin lines of intersection repeated again and again. Although much reduced in size they still preserve the diamond form. When viewed from another angle they appear to be square in the center.

A small star is sometimes cut on the face of each octagon. Other small designs are seen on them, but this extra ornamentation is generally very weak.

If the cutter is to make a "round hollow" on a punch bowl, he moves the bowl in a gentle rocking motion on the iron or stone wheel. While easing it in a horizontal direction he must watch the growing size of the hollow. This round hollow may be made on the proper wheel with scarcely a movement of the glass.

Flowers are cut on the "flute" wheel and because the buds are not round they are rolled into shape first.

The "panel" wheel takes part in the ornamentation of many pieces. The wheel may be narrower than three-eighths of an inch but is seldom any wider. Edge cuts which are usually found around flower leaves are generally done on the edge of the "panel" wheel. Small intersecting cuts in the center of the flower are put in with a small mitre wheel. The same type of wheel is usually used for cuts around the outside of the flower and for other edge cuts. The stems of the flowers may be put in with the same wheel or with one which is slightly rounder. The edge of the "panel" wheel may also be used for marking off equal distances with perpendicular lines which may rise in a raised mitre design.

The scallops which appear in a variety of shapes on the edges of glass are cut with the "mitre" wheel. The corners are then trimmed off with the stone wheel until they take on a circular form.

The "mandril" is sometimes used by the glass

cutter when very fine work or difficult parts of a pattern make it necessary. This particular type of mandril is quite similar to today's hand-held electric drill. The original glass cutters say that its use makes Glass Cutting and the Art of Engraving a single profession. As cut glass developed commercially, the alliance of the mandril with the spindle became more rapid, until today the two types of cutting are spoken of as one.

A diaper design of facet with facet and prism with prism all over the body of a jug, decanter or the bowl of a wine glass, was generally what the glass cutter liked to do most of all. While cutting a line, the wheel lent itself freely to the cutter's continuing it as far as the vessel allowed; either up or down, horizontally or diagonally. The natural tendency was to repeat this operation by crossing and recrossing the line. The apparent result was that the patterns were too geometrical and lacked variety. If the cutter did not possess the Art faculty he could rarely encourage it in face of the limitations offered by the material and equipment.

While the main thought was to increase the brilliancy of the article's effect; there came to be more important problems such as the fuller idealizing of flowers and fruits. Cutters of taste began to find it possible to place the prism, in all its cut-glass variety, into flowers and fruits in the glass. They were thus able to bring light in all its colors into their work. It was through this upward drive for more artistic effects that the cutter was able to enhance the natural tone or purity of the best flint glass from which all good cut glass was made.

The beauty of the various patterns depended generally upon the ideas of the cutter and the quality of his taste along with the proper command of his tools.

Glass cutting did not offer as wide an opportunity for inventive genius or artistically finished work as the more pliable field of glass engraving and carving. From its beginning, the Art improved, and during the height of its popularity was brought into harmony with the educated taste of the time and became the fashion of its day.

ACHILLES

Plate.—Achilles pattern.

Plate - 7 inches.

Celery Tray.—Achilles.

ACHILLES - continued

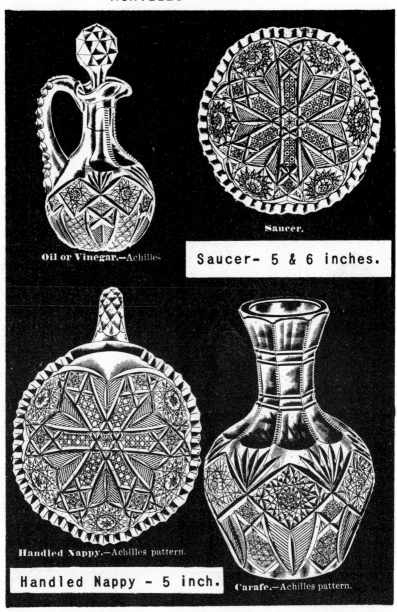

Oil or Vinegar.—Achilles

Saucer.

Saucer- 5 & 6 inches.

Handled Nappy.—Achilles pattern.

Handled Nappy - 5 inch.

Carafe.—Achilles pattern.

ACHILLES – continued

Cream Pitcher.—Achilles pattern.

Sugar Bowl.—Achilles pattern to match above.

ADAMS

Berry Nappy

ALBION

Punch Bowl - 10 inches.

ALPHA

Bon Bon or Olive Dish.

ALPINE

Vase - 8 inch.

ARCADIA

Bell - Hgt. 4½ inches.

ARIEL

Jug - 3 pints.

ASTORIA

Bowl - 8 inch.

AUBURN

Bon Bon or Olive Dish - 6 x 6 inches.

25

AVON

Cream Pitcher

Sugar Bowl - Hgt. $3\frac{1}{2}$ inches.

AVON - continued

Handled Nappy - 6 inches.

AVONDALE

Bowl - 8 inch.

AZALIA

Vase - 8 & 10 inches.

BEVERLY

Sugar and Cream Set

BRILLIANT

Mayonnaise Set

Fern Dish
8 inches.

BUZZ

Jug

CAMBRIDGE

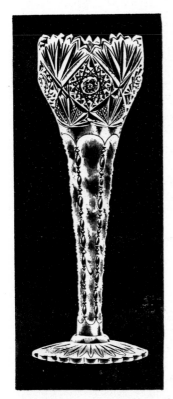

Lemonade or Punch Cup

Vase - 8 inch

Cigarette or Tobacco Jar -Hgt. 5 $\frac{1}{4}$ inches.

CECIL

Bowl - 8 inch.

SIDE LIGHT ON CUT GLASS DESIGN

Much of the early 1900 Cut Glass was more or less copied from those of the period 1800-1830, popularly called Waterford. The use of steam engines to drive the cutting machines led the glass cutters to sacrifice the natural blown glass forms of glass for the sake of a masterly display of deep and accurate cutting. Glasses became too deeply and profusely cut, emitting a blaze of prismatic light, but having an unpleasantly rough surface. The worst types produced were early Victorian. John Ruskin, impressed with the vulgarity of these glasses, wrote a sweeping condemnation of all Cut Glass. For a time this brought the craft into discredit and undoubtedly injured the English glass trade. Decoration by cutting almost disappeared for a time. At this time glass cutters were moving forward in the United States and they began to develop new and much finer pieces of glass than any turned out by other countries. Cut Glass recovered its former popularity and America went on to lead the world in the production of fine Cut Glassware.

CHRYSANTHEMUM

Bowl - 8 & 9 inch.

Oval Ice Cream Tray.—Chrysanthemum pattern.

COLONIAL

Cigar Jar

COLUMBIA

Spoon Tray

CORONA

Tumbler

Water Set - 14 inch mirror.

CREST

Sugar and Cream Set

CRESTON

Mayonnaise Set

CUMBERLAND

Vase - 8 & 10 inch.

CYCLONE

Lemonade Cup

CYRANO

Bowl.—Cyrano pattern.

Saucer - 5 & 6 inch.

Oil or Vinegar - Hgt. $7\frac{1}{4}$ inches.

CYRANO – continued

Berry Nappy – 7 inch.

DELPHI

Tumbler

Pitcher - 3 pints.

DIANA

Goblet

Vase - 8 & 10 inches.

Ice Tub.—Diana pattern.

41

DIANA – continued

Cordial.

Claret.

Champagne.

Sherry.

Wine.

EDNA

Jug - 3½ pints.

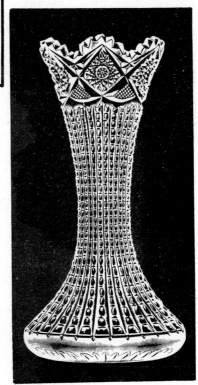

ELBA

Vase - 10 inch.

ELECTRIC

Whisky Glass

ESTELLA

Jelly Nappy.
Estella pattern. rolled top.

Jelly Nappy - 6 inch.

EVANSTON

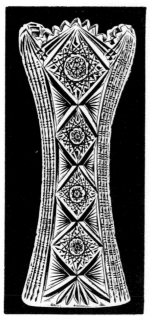

Cigar Jar - Hgt. 7¾ inches.

Vase - 8 & 10 inches.

FLEMISH

Bon Bon or Olive Dish

FLORENTINE

Cigar Jar

Bowl - 7-8-9-10 inches.

FORTUNA

Water Set

Sugar and Cream Set

Mayonnaise Set   Footed Bowl - 8 inches.

FORTUNA - continued

J ug - 4 pints.

Spoon Holder

Fern Dish

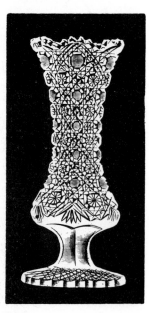

Vase - 8-10-12-14 inches.

FRISCO HOB

Jug

FULDA

Oil or Vinegar

GARFIELD

Berry Nappy
7-8-9 inches.

GENOA

Punch Bowl
9 inches.

GLENWOOD

Tumbler

Carafe

Rose Ball - 5 & 6 inch.

HARVARD

Violet Vase

FLINT GLASS

Flint Glass is a species of glass made of white sand, 52; carbonate of lead, 33; alumina, I; with metallic additions to neutralize the color making it clear and thus giving it the name of Crystal glass. Pure white sand free from oxide of iron is required for flint glass, as iron imparts a green color. The sand for its manufacture was formerly derived from pulverized flints, and that gave it the name of flint glass. The presence of lead gives it a peculiar property of refracting light, which causes it to be used for cut glass dishes. It has less color, owing to the use of alkali potash instead of soda, the latter imparting a greenish tinge to glass. Flint glass is also softer than many other varieties, and this makes it the finest for cutting into tableware, bottles, and various articles of decorative furniture and

HOLLY WREATH

Bon Bon or Olive Dish

Lemonade or Punch Cup

Saucer - 5 & 6 inch.

HUDSON

Jug

HURON

Celery Tray

INDIA

Plate - 12 inches

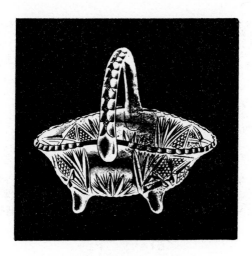

Bonbon Basket

IOWA

Spoon Tray

IRIS

Mayonnaise Set

IRVING

Comport - 6 & 7 inch

IVY

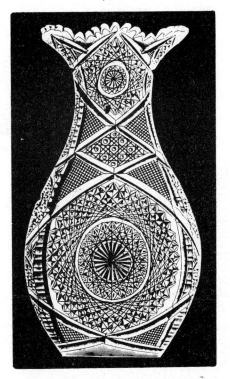

Vase - 8 & 10 inch.

KENMORE

Mayonnaise Bowl

Sugar
and
Cream Set

LAPIDARY

Knife Rest - $4\frac{1}{2}$ & $4\frac{3}{4}$ inches.

Tooth Pick Holder

LAUREL WREATH

Berry Nappy - 7 & 8 inch.

Pickle Dish - 8 inch.

LAUREL WREATH - continued

Handled Wine Decanter.   Unhandled Wine Decanter.

Celery Tray.—Laurel Wreath pattern.

LAUREL WREATH – continued

Finger Bowl

Bon Bon or Olive Dish

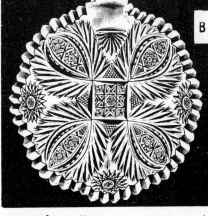

Handled Nappy - 5 & 6 inch.

Oil or Vinegar

Sugar and Cream Set

LAUREL WREATH - continued

Tumbler

Bowl - 7 & 8 inch.

Whisky Jug

Cologne

LEDA

Celery Tray

LESSING

Sugar

and

Cream Set

LIBERTY

Bowl - 7-9-10 inches.

LIBERTY BUZZ

Goblet   Tumbler

LIBERTY HOBB

Tumbler

LINCOLN

Jug - 4 pints.

LIPMAN

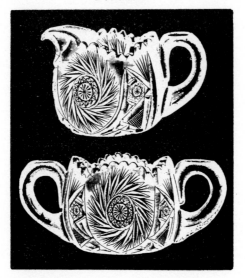

Sugar and Cream Set

A Mitre Wheel

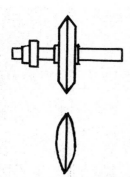

A mitre wheel is shaped as in the drawing. These are found in all sizes and make incisions the shape of a leaf, as shown here. The wheel here is represented on its spindle. The two ends of the shaft are held, when in motion, in wooden blocks which may be adjusted as the work requires.

LOTUS

Handled Nappy - 5 inch.

Bon Bon or Olive Dish

Saucer - 5 inch.

LUNAR

Wine Decanter - 1 quart.

LYNN

Plate - 7 inches.

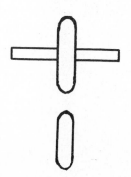

A Fluting Wheel

This wheel is rounded off on the face as shown here and is used for "flute" cuts which, if done on a square surface of glass resemble it in form as is here viewed. This is the wheel that is used for hollowing out circles.

LYRIC

Bowl - 7 & 8 inch.

Dressing Bowl and Plate

LYRIC - continued

Mayonnaise Bowl - quart.

Violet Ball - Hgt. 2 $\frac{3}{4}$ inches.

Violet Ball and Plateau

MAINE

Bowl

MANILA

Sugar and Cream Set

MARCY

Comport

MARION

Oil or Vinegar

MASCOT

Bon Bon or Olive Dish

MAYFLOWER

Oval Dish - 7 x 11½ inches.

METEOR

Bowl - 7 & 8 inch.

Handled Nappy   Olive Dish

Celery Tray

METEOR - continued

Finger Bowl

Wine Decanter

Carafe

Sugar and Cream Set

METEOR - continued

Tumbler

Flower Centre - 8-10-12 inches.

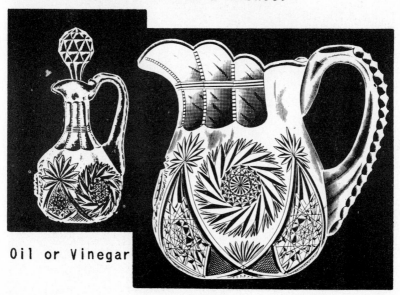

Oil or Vinegar

Pitcher - 3 pints.

MOGUL

Tumbler

Pitcher - 3 pints.

MYRTLE WREATH

Bon Bon or Olive Dish

A Split Cut Wheel

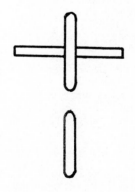

Here is a split cut wheel which has the same shape as a fluting wheel but is much narrower. With this shape the incision can be made much deeper into the surface. The split cut is deeper in the middle than on the sides but has a rounded bottom instead of the V-shaped channel made by the mitre wheel.

NILES

Plate - 7 inches.

Spoon Tray

Sugar and Cream Set

NILES – continued

Bowl – 7 & 8 inch.

Oil or Vinegar   Pitcher

NILES – continued

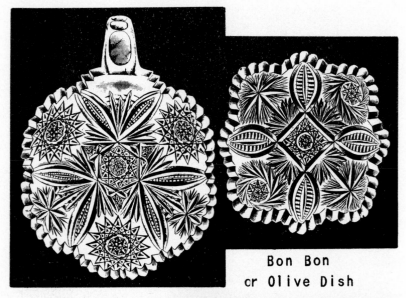

Bon Bon
cr Olive Dish

Handled Nappy

Tumbler

Carafe

NORDICA

Nut Bowl - 8 inch.

OLD ENGLISH

Bowl - 9 inches.

Handled Nappy - 6 inches

ORION

Bowl - 9 inches.

The Panel Wheel

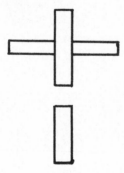

The panel wheel is similar to the split cut wheel, except that its face is flat on the surface like the illustration. As one can see its cut is sharp-edged like itself. This wheel is used for cutting panels and for various cuts in glass decoration where end cuts are needed.

OROMONDE

Pitcher

ORPHEUS

Saucer - 5 inch.

OZONE

Plate - 12 inches

Covered Butter Dish

Cheese Dish

Sugar and Cream Set

Carafe

OZONE – continued

Ice Cream Tray

Two-handled Relish Dish

Ice Tub

Comport   Decanter

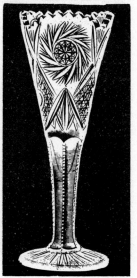

Vase

OZONE - continued

Bowl

Mayonnaise Set
Tall.

Mayonnaise Set

Two-handled nappy

Handled Nappy - 6 inches.

Celery Tray

OZONE BUZZ'

Jug - 3 pints.

PALACE

Bowl - 8 inch.

PALMETTO WREATH

Whisky Glass

PARAGON

Handled Nappy - 6 inches.

PILGRIM

Jelly Nappy - 6 inch.

PLYMOUTH

Nappy - 7 & 8 inches.

Comport

Handled Nappy

PREMIER

Handled Nappy - 5 inch.

RADIUM

Bowl

Mitre Wheel Design

Prismy "diamond" patterns are cut by the mitre wheel. These cuts are placed up against the sides of other mitre cuts and this makes the sides angular instead of circular. Here are some of the better known patterns that cutters develop by such mitre work.

RAMBLER

Punch Bowl, Footed - 10-12-14 inch.

Oval Ice Cream Tray

RAMBLER ~ continued

Oil or Vinegar

Handled Nappy - 5 inch.

Water Set

RAMBLER - continued

Berry Nappy

Sugar and Cream Set   Whisky Jug

RAMBLER - continued

Bowl - 7 & 8 inch.

Bon Bon
or Olive Dish

Pitcher

REGENT

Handled Nappy - 6 inches.

ROY

Ice Tub and Plate

ROYAL

Bon Bon or Olive Dish

RUSTIC

Berry Nappy - 7-8-9 inches.

SABINE

Footed Bon Bon Dish

Octagon Diamond Design

This is one of the most popular types of cut glass. If the four points of the first diagram are cut away to an equal length with the sides that remain, an eight-sided figure remains. When this figure is repeated over and over it not only preserves the diamond form but it also contains the square.

ST. LOUIS

Finger Bowl

Catsup

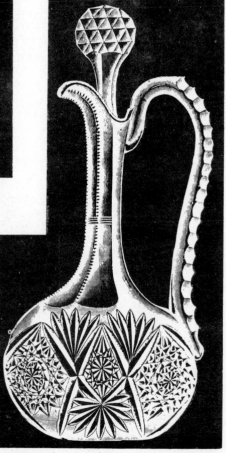

Goblet   Handled-Wine Decanter

ST. LOUIS - continued

Champagne   Claret   Sherry

Wine Set - 1 quart.

SARDIS

Water Set

Tumbler

Bon Bon
or Olive Dish

Oil or Vinegar

SERVIA

Tumblers

Carafe

SIDNEY

Spoon Tray

103

SPARTA

Celery Tray

Scallops

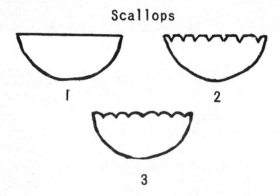

Scallops are cut out of the plain lip of the bowl or goblet base by incisions made at equal distances apart with a mitre wheel. Starting with a blank bowl (1) and using the iron mitre wheel the sharp-edged cuts are made in the rim (2). These top square corners are trimmed round with a stone wheel until they take the circular form as seen in (3). There are many variations of scallops possible but the cutting procedure is always the same.

STARLING

Bowl - 8 inch.

Tumbler

Pitcher

STARLING – continued

Oil or Vinegar

Carafe

Water Set

STERLING

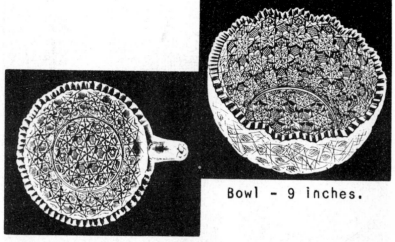

Bowl - 9 inches.

Handled Nappy - 6 inches.

TEXAS

Bon Bon or Olive Dish

TROY

Bon Bon
or Olive Dish

Claret Pitcher

Sugar
and
Cream Set

TROY – continued

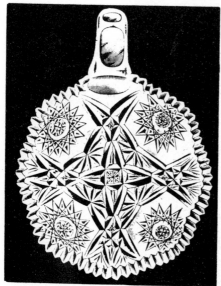

Handled Nappy

Oil or Vinegar

Tumbler

Pitcher

TROY - continued

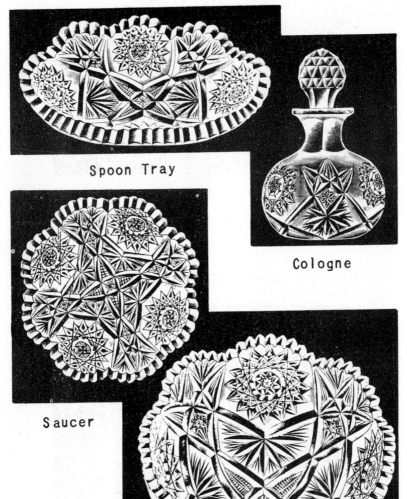

Spoon Tray

Cologne

Saucer

Bowl - 7 & 8 inch.

VICTOR

Spoon Tray

VICTORIA

Bowl - 8-9-10 inches.

VIOLA

Sugar and Cream Set

WALTHAM

Bowl - 9 inches.

WALTON

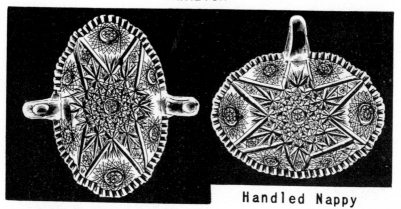

Two-handled dish   Handled Nappy

WINDSOR

Berry Nappy – 7-8-9 inches.

INDEX

Achilles, 19-21
Adams, 22
Albion, 22
Alpha, 23
Alpine, 23
Arcadia, 24
Ariel, 24
Astoria, 25
Auburn, 25
Avon, 26, 27
Avondale, 27
Azalia, 28
Beverly, 29
Brilliant, 30
Buzz, 30
Cambridge, 31
Cecil, 32
Chrysanthemum, 33
Colonial, 34
Columbia, 34
Corona, 35
Crest, 36
Creston, 36
Cut Glass, History,
    7-10
Cumberland, 37
Cyclone, 37
Cyrano, 38, 39
Delphi, 40
Diana, 41, 42
Edna, 43
Elba, 43
Electric, 44
Estella, 44
Evanston, 45
Flemish, 45
Flint Glass, 52
Florentine, 46
Fluting Wheel, 69
Fortuna, 47, 48
Frisco Hob, 49
Fulda, 49
Garfield, 50
Genoa, 50
Glass Cutting, 11-18
Glenwood, 51
Harvard, 52
History, Cut Glass, 7-10
Holly Wreath, 53
Hudson, 54
Huron, 54
India, 55
Iowa, 56
Iris, 56
Irving, 56
Ivy, 57
Kenmore, 58
Lapidary, 58

Laurel Wreath, 59-62
Leda, 63
Lessing, 63
Liberty, 64
Liberty Buzz, 64
Liberty Hobb, 65
Lincoln, 65
Lipman, 66
Lotus, 67
Lunar, 68
Lynn, 69
Lyric, 70, 71
Maine, 72
Manila, 72
Marcy, 73
Marion, 73
Mascot, 74
Mayflower, 74
Meteor, 75-77
Mitre Wheel, 66
Mitre Wheel Design, 92
Mogul, 78
Myrtle Wreath, 79
Niles, 80-82
Nordica, 83
Octagon Diamond Design,
    99
Old English, 83
Orion, 84
Oromonde, 85
Orpheus, 85
Ozone, 86-88
Ozone Buzz, 89
Palace, 89
Palmetto Wreath, 89
Panel Wheel, 84
Paragon, 90
Pilgrim, 90
Plymouth, 91
Premier, 91
Radium, 92
Rambler, 93-96
Regent, 97
Roy, 97
Royal, 98
Rustic, 98
Sabine, 99
St. Louis, 100, 101
Sardis, 102
Scallops, 104
Servia, 103
Side Light on Cut
    Glass Design, 32
Sidney, 103
Sparta, 104
Split Cut Wheel, 79
Starling, 105, 106
Sterling, 107

INDEX, Continued

Texas, 107
Troy, 108-110
Victor, 111
Victoria, 111

Viola, 112
Waltham, 112
Walton, 113
Windsor, 113

Crouch

WITHDRAWN